Past struggles
Current fights

Each year women delegates representing trade unions and workplaces from across Scotland meet at the annual STUC Women's Conference and STUC Congress. The agendas give snapshots of the different trade unions, industries and the experiences of women workers from the past, from which we can learn and should be inspired. The above examples are from the STUC Archive.

Introduction

In March 2011, the STUC Women's Committee marked the 100th anniversary of International Women's Day by inviting women from trade unions and other organisations to join a celebration at the STUC building in Glasgow. Through sharing memories, photographs, campaign badges and other memorabilia we soon realised that there was much to record. The project "Inspiring Women" took shape. Members of the STUC Women's Committee, past and present, have worked with Carole McCallum, Archivist at the STUC Archives, Glasgow Caledonian University, and others, to bring together some of the stories of the women who have shaped the labour movement in Scotland today.

"Inspiring Women" does not set out to be a history of women and the Scottish trade union movement, nor is it the complete story of the STUC Women's Committee. The content comes from some of the suggestions made by those who contributed to the project. It provides snapshots which seek to give voice to women in Scotland and their struggles for equality and justice, from which we benefit today. We hope that the images will bring back memories and encourage everyone to talk with their families, in communities and workplaces, about the contribution working women made, and will continue to make. Some of the sources for further research are listed at the back of the book.

Women have long campaigned to improve conditions of employment, and for equality in pay and treatment in the workplace. However, history also records that women active in the trade union movement and wider labour movement spoke up strongly for good housing, for fair rents, for childcare, for a health service which took full account of the needs of women and children, against violence against women, for universal suffrage, and for equal representation, whether in political or trade union arenas. These campaigns spread beyond the local communities in which women lived, to the shop floors and factory gates, building solidarity with workers in England, Ireland and Wales, and travelling further afield.

For the STUC, commitments to equal pay for women, and to women being able to vote, were expressed at the founding Conferences. By 1926, the STUC had established a Women's Advisory Committee and a Conference was held that year for 'unions with female members or those affected by the organisation of women workers'. With each year that passed, more women organised and became involved.

The STUC Women's Committee assumed a more statutory position, and during the 1980s and 1990s changes were made which included agreeing reserved seats for women, and incorporating women's representation across most of the structures of the STUC. Every second year the STUC President is a woman delegate.

Women now make up nearly half of the organised trade union movement in Scotland, and are in the majority in a number of sectors. In 2011, for the first time, more women than men were elected to the STUC's governing body, the General Council.

The STUC Women's Committee continues to make common cause with other women's organisations in wider society. At the time of writing, we are approaching a referendum on independence in Scotland which will be held in September 2014. The approach taken by the STUC has been to encourage maximum participation and debate on our view of "A Just Scotland". Whatever the outcome of the constitutional debate, it is a certainty that there will be a need for women to continue to organise, and to speak up.

In learning from the past, we gain ideas and energy for the future, so let us treasure those memories, and take inspiration from the role played by women in some of those campaigns, political events and movements for change.

Ann Henderson

Ann Henderson, STUC Assistant Secretary
Secretary to STUC Women's Committee April 2013

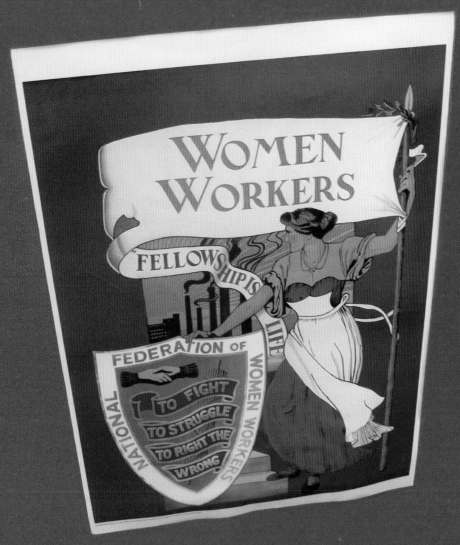

Mary Macarthur, born in Glasgow in 1880, campaigned passionately in Scotland and in London for better conditions for women workers, including homeworkers. She organised strikes, set up trade boards, and agreed minimum wage rates. In 1906 she became National Secretary of the National Federation of Women Workers, which in Scotland alone had a membership of around 2,000 women prior to World War I. Mary Macarthur founded the 'Women Worker' monthly paper. The image on the NFWW banner was taken from the illustrated cover of the journal, designed by Walter Crane.

Margaret Irwin
1858 - 1940

A trade union and suffrage
activist, Margaret Hardings Irwin
was born at sea on 13 January 1858.
In 1891, she began her lifetime's
work on improving working
women's conditions.

Margaret became the full-time organising secretary of the
Women's Protective and Provident League, a philanthropic
organisation sponsored by the Glasgow Trades Council.
In 1895, she became secretary of the Scottish Council for
Women's Trades (SCWT) and continued in this role for
44 years. By 1895, the SCWT represented 100,000 members
affiliated to 16 Trades Councils.

On 25 March 1897, the first Scottish Trade Union Congress
was held in Glasgow. Those on the platform included
Margaret Irwin, who was secretary of the arrangements
committee. She was subsequently unanimously appointed
as secretary of the Congress. In Margaret's first speech to
Congress, she successfully moved the motion on women's
suffrage.

WOMEN'S SUFFRAGE.

Miss IRWIN moved:—

"That, in view of the important legislative measures relating to the social and industrial conditions of women which are at present before the country, it is desirable to allow women a direct voice in the making of the laws which so seriously affect them, by extending the parliamentary franchise to women on the same footing as to men." She remarked that she had always believed in women's suffrage, but until she came to be associated with the labour movement, it was more a pious opinion with her than a living faith. Since she had come to work in this movement, it seemed to her the first thing women had to work for. Trade Unionism, good as it was, had its limits, and they must apply legislation to the remedy of women's grievances, for the reason that it was so extremely difficult to get women to organise. She would rather organise ten men's Unions than one women's Union. It was not the fault of the women—it was the fault of their conditions. This question of women's suffrage should not be allowed to become a party question. It was a woman's question, and the woman's party was big enough to include all parties. She felt if this question was anything at all it was a labour question. She had always felt that, because so much of the legislation of to-day dealt with industrial and social questions in which women had as great a stake as men. The pressure of the time was driving more and more women into the labour market. She quite agreed that women ought to work at anything that was suitable; the only thing that she objected to was their taking men's work at 50 per cent. of their wages. Among the objections urged against women's suffrage was that women did not care to have a vote, and that they were quite indifferent. She thought that was a mistaken idea; but in any case there were many men who did not vote, and yet it was not contended that they should abolish the franchise for them.

Mr JOHN KEIR, Aberdeen Trade Council, seconded the resolution.

Mr JOHN JACK, Alva, moved that they add after the word " desirable " "as a matter of right."

Mr JOHNSTON, Motherwell, seconded, and Miss Irwin having accepted the addition, the resolution was adopted.

Extract from Margaret Irwin's first speech to Scottish Trade Union Congress 1897

7

STUC Congress 1911

**Women left to right
Jeanie Spence
Mrs Lamont
Agnes Brown
Mary Macarthur
Kate McLean and
Rachel Devine**

This is the first known photograph of the women delegates to the STUC Congress, apart from Margaret Irwin who represented the Scottish Council of Women's Trades. This photograph appeared in the Dundee Advertiser of 27 April 1911 titled "Ladies of STUC in Dundee". Apart from giving the names of the delegates there was no other accompanying text. However, the importance of these delegates to women in the Scottish trade union movement is considerable, and thereafter the STUC was never without women delegates.

The two delegates on the left and right were representing the Dundee Jute and Flax Workers' Union established in 1906. Three out of four workers in jute mills were women and 75% of Dundee's working women were employed there. The four central delegates, including the National Leader and General Secretary, Mary Macarthur, represent the National Federation of Women Workers, founded in 1906. Born in Glasgow, Mary became one of the most outstanding women of the trade union and labour movement. Beside her is Kate McLean, who was elected onto the parliamentary committee of the STUC and two years later played a key role in organising the Kilbirnie Net Workers' strike.

Timelines

1866 – First petition by women for the right to vote
presented in the House of Commons
Suffrage society started in Edinburgh

1870 - First Women's Suffrage Bill rejected by Parliament

1897 – National Union of Women's Suffrage Societies
formed (suffragists)

1903 – Women's Social and Political Union (WSPU)
formed (suffragettes)

1906 – Dr Elsie Inglis launched her Scottish Women's
Suffrage Movement in Edinburgh

1908 – Scottish HQ of WSPU opened in Glasgow

1909 – Marion Wallace Dunlop, a WSPU member
from Scotland, is imprisoned in Holloway
and goes on hunger strike

1909 – Pageant in Edinburgh

1914 - On declaration of war WSPU suspends actions

1918 – The Representation of the People Act

1918 – The Parliamentary Qualification of Women Act
(enabled women to stand as MPs)

1918 – Eunice Murray stood in the General Election
(as an Independent in Glasgow, Bridgeton) –
first woman to do so

1919 – Lady Astor (1879-1964) became first woman MP
(for Plymouth South) to take her seat in the House
of Commons

1928 – The Equal Franchise Act - women have the vote on
the same basis as men.

Women's suffrage procession

A Women's suffrage procession took place
in Edinburgh on 10 October 1909. The event
was organised by the Women's Social and
Political Union (WSPU), and focused on the
achievements of women in the past and the
opportunities for women in the future. This
photograph shows the procession advancing
along Princes Street, Edinburgh. This postcard
image comes from Ellen Gorrie's photographic
album held in the National Library of Scotland.
Ellen Gorrie joined the WSPU around 1908 and
played the prized part of Mary, Queen of Scots,
in the 1909 procession.

(Reproduced by kind permission of the National Library of Scotland.)

In 1911, the Singer Sewing machine company employed 11,500 workers in the Kilbowie factory, Clydebank. Approximately 50% of the young women in Clydebank worked for Singer's. Piece rates, time and motion studies, and management's search for ever more efficient work practices at the expense of the workforce, dominated the factory regime. In 1911, the factory closed in a dispute provoked by management adding additional work onto a group of 12 women with no additional pay. By the end of the day, 10,000 workers had walked out in solidarity. The dispute ended a couple of weeks later, with management threatening to move the work abroad. Hundreds of workers were victimised, including all the strike leaders and known union

Jane Rae was actively involved in the strike - for which she was sacked. She joined the Independent Labour Party after hearing Keir Hardie. She was a suffragette, once chairing an Emily Pankhurst meeting in Clydebank Town Hall. She was politically active in the anti-war campaign in 1914, the Cooperative movement and the temperance movement. From 1922 to 1928, she was a local Councillor and became a J.P. with a fierce reputation when dealing with any man who mistreated his wife.

In 2012, the Glasgow Women's Library and Clydebank Women's History Group secured agreement for a memorial to Jane Rae in the Clydebank Town Hall - a welcome recognition of the contribution made by Jane and others of her

Women at Burnbank Cross soup kitchen in Hamilton, Lanarkshire, during the General Strike in 1926.

Bob Smillie, M.P., an ex-miner himself, and a member of the General Council, had Congress in tears with an emotional appeal for a redoubled effort to collect funds for the miners and their families. "I have seen", his great voice boomed out, "in every mining town and village—I have seen this myself in some places—where the husband might, because of the home conditions, be showing weakness; I have heard their women say: 'Not a step! There must be no return until there is a satisfactory settlement. . . .'"

"HUMAN RIGHTS"

Man holds so exquisitely tight
    To everything he deems his right;
If woman wants a share, to fight
    She has, and strive with all her might.

But we are nothing like so jealous
    As any of our surly fellows;
Give us our rights and we'll not care
    To cheat our brothers of their share.

Above such selfish *man-like* frights,
    We'd give fair play, let come what might,
To he or she folk, black or white,
    And haste the reign of Human Right.

            Marion Bernstein,
       From Mirren's Musings, 1876.

Membership card for the West of Scotland Power Loom Female Weavers' Society, 1833.

13

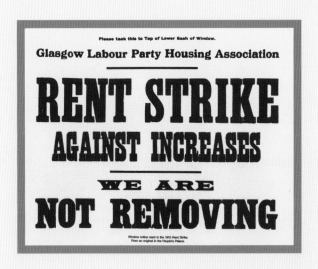

Please tack this to Top of Lower Sash of Window.

Glasgow Labour Party Housing Association

RENT STRIKE
AGAINST INCREASES
WE ARE
NOT REMOVING

Window notice used in the 1915 Rent Strike.
From an original in the People's Palace.

World War I began in July 1914. The Munitions Act brought wage controls, but prices still kept rising. In the cities, working people were housed in overcrowded, bad quality housing. The private landlords started imposing rent increases, and communities organised in response. The Glasgow Women's Housing Association, and other local housing associations, supported families facing eviction with community campaigns to drive out Sheriff's Officers. Drums, bells, trumpets or indeed anything that could be used to create a warning sound rallied help. The women would cram into closes and doorways to stop evictions going ahead. Public meetings were held at the gates of the shipyards and factories.

On 17 November 1915, a number of tenants were due to appear at Glasgow Sheriff Court for refusal to pay rent increases. Strikes and solidarity came from thousands of shipyard and engineering workers, and a huge demonstration of women, children and men filled the city centre. The rights of landlords to set whatever rent level they wished was challenged successfully. Protests spread across Scotland and to other cities in England and Wales, and on 23 December 1915, the Rent and Mortgage Interest (War Restrictions) Act received Royal Assent. This was a great victory, and one for which women and their communities could claim full credit.

MARY BARBOUR

One of the strongest voices in the South Govan Women's Housing Association, set up in 1915, was Mary Barbour. One of the largest demonstrations ever seen in Glasgow was in November of that year, when thousands of women, led by Mary, accompanied by shipyard and engineering workers, converged on the Sheriff Court. The action spread around the country. In the local Govan community, "Mrs Barbour's Army", drove out Sheriffs Officers and resisted evictions.

Mary Barbour was a member of the Co-op Women's Guild and the Independent Labour Party. In 1920, she became the first woman to be a Labour Councillor in Glasgow, representing Govan Fairfield ward. She also became a baillie. As a councillor, she campaigned for municipal banks, washhouses, laundries and baths, pure milk supplied free to children, child welfare centres and play areas, home helps, and pensions for mothers. She pioneered the city's first family planning centre. Mary lived until 1958, supporting good causes to the end. Since 2012, the STUC Women's Committee has given its support to a rapidly growing campaign for full recognition of the significant contribution Mary made to the rent strikes campaign, to the city of Glasgow, and to improving the lives of women and their families.

The Herring Lassies

Gutters at work Wick

The Herring Lassies from Scotland organised across the UK.

At the beginning of the 20th century, the Scottish herring industry was the biggest fishery in the world and a major contributor to both the Highland and Scottish economy. Crucial to the industry were the thousands of herring lassies, many from the Highlands and Islands, who gutted and packed the fish.

The women went where the herring went, following the 'silver darlings' from Shetland to Lowestoft. It's quite staggering to picture this army of women travelling the length and breadth of the UK in the early 1900s, often on specially commissioned trains.

In 1914, the Scottish Fishworkers' Friendly Society ~~~ted 4,000 herring workers

which included coopers and carters as well as the women. Reports highlight strike action in Shetland in 1929 which saw the end of six women having to share a hut (it was changed to three). In 1931, there were mass meetings in Peterhead and Stornoway protesting over wages and a summer strike in Barra in 1935, also over wages.

One of the most reported strikes took place in Yarmouth in 1936, and involved 4,000 'Scots Fisher Lassies' withdrawing their labour. Mounted police had to be called in to patrol the streets. The women, however, did not give in. The women were paid 10d per barrel of gutted and packed herring (shared between the group of three). Following the strike, the rate was increased to 12d (a shilling) per barrel.

8 Day and Week-End Schools for Women Trade Unionists.—It was reported to the 1938 Annual Conference that the holding of week-end schools for the purpose of instructing women trade unionists had become an annual feature of the Committee's activities. In continuance of this practice we arranged the Fifth Week-End School on 25th and 26th March, 1939, and the Sixth Week-End School on 25th and 26th May, 1940. Both Schools were held at Stirling. The particulars with regard to them are:—

1939 School.—The subjects selected were "The Development of Trade Unionism" and "The Industries of Scotland," the former being an historical survey of the growth of Trade Unionism, and the latter being a description of the Industries of Scotland and the Trade Unions within them. The Lecturer was Councillor Wm. Elger, J.P. 51 students were in attendance from 11 Unions.

1940 School.—The subjects selected for this School were "The Development of Trade Unionism" (Lecturer, Miss Betty Lamont), and "The War-Time Activities of the Unions" (Lecturer, Councillor Wm. Elger, J.P.). 42 students were in attendance from 9 Unions.

The STUC Women's Committee has continued to hold popular Weekend Schools, with Committee members themselves delivering courses on topics such as "Women into Public Life"; and "Conference Skills". In September 2012, the STUC Women's Committee held a Women's Weekend School on "Understanding Economics". This was delivered jointly with the "Women in Scotland's Economy" team from Glasgow Caledonian University. During the sessions, participants looked at their jobs paid and unpaid, what was already known about economics, women in Scotland's economy, feminist economics, and how to get more women talking about the economy. Everyone who attended the school gained an insight into economics, how women are viewed in the economy, and the language used by economists.

OUR WORLD

Scottish trade union women have a proud history of global solidarity with women on issues such as human rights, dignity equality and freedom. A common sense of mission drives us and millions of others around the world to pursue justice and inclusion. Women's struggles have coincided with deep changes in our world, from protests against inequality, to uprisings for freedom and democracy.

We have shown solidarity and support for sisters and brothers in Chile, Colombia, Palestine and South Africa to mention but a few. The role played by women in the struggle against apartheid was acknowledged by Nelson Mandela when he said: "I pay tribute to the mothers and wives and sisters of our Nation. You are the rock hard foundation of our struggle."

In highlighting the significant work done by women in international struggle, we also need to underline the role of women to ensure their increased representation in the prevention and resolution of conflicts and in peace-building. The participation of women is essential for establishing constructive dialogue with all interested parties and for accommodating all gender-specific concerns at all stages of any conflict.

Trade union sponsored international solidarity has produced effective results and continues to assist in the release of men and women jailed in countries such as Colombia, for so-called terrorist activities. Colombia, at the time of writing, is still the most dangerous country in which to be a trade unionist. International solidarity secured the release of Liliany Obando who was imprisoned for more than three and a half years in Buen Pastor Prison, Bogota.

Liliany was never brought to trial during the time she spent in prison. I visited Liliany in prison in Bogota and was impressed by the courage and determination of all the women imprisoned for simply being a trade unionist. The struggle continues for those political prisoners that remain behind bars.

Scottish trade union women have a special bond with their sisters in Palestine and exchange visits are organised despite the difficulties imposed by the Israeli Government. We promote and encourage the purchase of Palestinian women's produce and products at all of our conferences and events. We also support the STUC campaign for a boycott of Israeli goods. Palestinian women who visit us in Scotland provide us with real inspiration and remind us of why we do what we do.

We have forged many relationships with many trade unionists in many countries, far too many to mention in this short contribution. Many advances have been made for women internationally.

As long as, however, the life expectancy of women in Zimbabwe is only 34 years, and it is cheaper to hire a woman than a donkey in India to carry heavy loads, then there remains still much to do.

Agnes Tolmie, UNITE, STUC President 2012 to 2013

CHILE

"How hard it is to sing
When I must sing of horror.
Horror which I am living,
Horror which I am dying.
To see myself among so much
and so many moments of infinity
in which silence and screams
are the end of my song.
What I see I have never seen.
What I have felt and what I feel
will give birth to the
moment........"

The above extract of the poem "National Stadium" was the final work of Victor Jara, poet, singer, songwriter, and loyal supporter of the Popular Unity Government of Chile, composed during his imprisonment in the Chile National Stadium in Santiago on 11 September 1973. Victor, along with thousands of other Chileans, was rounded up following the fascist coup on that day. Victor was brutally tortured and killed as were many other Chileans throughout Chile. On 18 of September, his wife Joan (a British subject) wrote:

"I had to go to the second floor which was the offices of the morgue and here also there were lines of bodies. And among these bodies I found Victor. A very battered, bloody body, half naked and full of machine gun wounds with his hands hanging from his wrists, his face bloody".

The overthrow of the young Popular Unity Government of Chile by the armed forces orchestrated by General Pinochet, showered havoc on the Chilean people and had wide reaching consequences throughout the world. Victor's story was just one of the many heartbreaking stories that was Chile under the rule of the military fascist dictatorship. In response to the terrible events in Chile, the National Chile Solidarity Committee, Chile Committee for Human Rights, the Refugee Committee and Cultural Groups were established. All branches of the same tree, making their own unique contribution of solidarity and friendship with the Chilean people.

The Scottish Chile Defence Committee and its Refugee Committee had strong support from the trade union and labour movement, including the STUC and its Women's Committee. The plight of Chilean women was raised at STUC Women's Conferences on numerous occasions. Delegates to the Women's Conference sent individual cards to Chilean women who were in prison. The purpose of this was twofold: to let the Prison authorities know that people in other countries were aware of the plight of Chilean women who were incarcerated without trial, and to show sisterhood to the women in Chile.

Chilean jewellery and handcrafted goods made by prisoners were sold at trade union women's events, including the Women's Conference, and money raising events were organised to raise funds for women in the shanty towns who were trying to feed their communities (a bit like the Women's Support Groups during the miners' strike in Britain). Similar action was taken in support of the families of political prisoners and of Chile's disappeared.

As a direct consequence of the Chilean struggle being raised at trade union events, including the Women's Conference, Chilean political prisoners were adopted by trade union branches. This was a very positive course of action and in some cases led to the release of the Chilean prisoner. One such case raised at the Women's Conference was that of the imprisonment of young Kelly Echiburu. Kelly and her family returned to Chile after living in Scotland as refugees. Kelly was arrested a couple of years after their return. There is no question that it was because of the national campaigning work, of which the STUC and Women's Committee was integral, that Kelly was released from prison.

In writing about solidarity with Chile, special mention must be made of the workers of Rolls Royce, East Kilbride, who refused to carry out repair work on the Chilean Hawker-Hunter Engines. This action was not only a moral boost to the progressive forces in Chile, it was one of the finest acts of international solidarity, applauded by trade unionists throughout the world.

There were innumerable acts of solidarity, not least of these being support for Chilean refugees who came to Scotland. Many refugees arriving in Scotland, were welcomed into, and stayed in the homes of labour and trade union activists before being housed by local governments in Scotland including Glasgow, Edinburgh, Dundee, Aberdeen, Clydebank, Dumbarton, Wishaw and Fife. And much of the house furnishings were donated by countless women and men who responded to the plight of the Chilean refugees. In conclusion, it was a privilege to be involved in solidarity action on Chile. Their optimism, music and art were all inspiring. We are indebted to the refugees who came to Scotland and to Chileans like Madam Allende and many others who represented all that was best in Chile and who touched and enriched our lives.

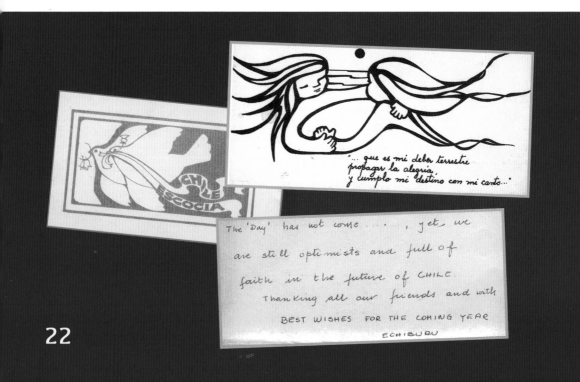

Equal Voice

SUMMER 1989   PRICE 20p

Palestine: women under occupation

PALESTINIAN women have made clear since the early days of the national struggle, their role in both society and politics. They equally suffer the oppression and injustice of their situation, and have campaigned equally with the men for their rights as Palestinians. This campaigning has taken on many forms from holding together their homes and families to working in the women's committees and being in the frontline of the Intifada. There are four women's committees which operate within the Occupied Territories of Palestine. They were formed in the early 1970's with the aim of providing health care, literacy classes, vocational training and child care facilities for Palestinian women and their families. The emphasis of the committees' projects has always been on self reliance — especially as all four committees are banned by the Israeli authorities.

Achievements

In the time in which these committees have been in operation, they have achieved a great deal — kindergartens, co-op workshops, literacy classes, family support networks, health clinics and even a health insurance scheme. They also started a campaign to make International Women's Day a paid holiday for women workers, and this has resulted in 500 institutes in the Occupied Territories agreeing to their demands.

Co-operative workshops

One new initiative of the women's committees is a pulse-based baby food based on chick peas and wheat. This product is very cheap compared to Israeli products, and also has a long shelf life — essential during the many curfews which camps and villages are placed under by the authorities. It is initiatives like these that the committees work on. Co-operative workshops are set up to make products for sale in the Occupied Territories which can replace the Israeli products and as such play a part in the aims of the Intifada.

Health care

Health care is a major problem in the Occupied Territories, and many projects have been set up by various organisations to try and ease the problem. In Jenin in Northern Palestine, the Patients Friends Society has set up a mother and baby clinic in its main polyclinic. This clinic serves a population of 170,000 people, and is obviously not enough to cope with the enormous demand. To help alleviate this problem, the society has set up a Village Outreach Project to cover outlying villages around the Jenin area. This project consists of 54 women who are trained in preventitive health care, and are then alloted a village each where they visit patients, checking on mothers and their children to check for regular growth etc. The only medicine these workers are allowed to give is Oral Rehydration Solution which is a simple mixture of sugar and water but can work miracles on a child suffering from dehydration and diarrhoea. These health workers can spot when something is not quite right and therefore ensure the patient gets to where they can be treated. However, 54 workers is not enough, and more are needed if the funding can be found.

We can help

We, as women in Scotland suffer the oppression of sexism in our society, but Palestinian women suffer the double oppression of occupation. As women trade unionists we can offer our solidarity to the women of Palestine in many ways — supporting projects, raising awareness, building links — but we can also learn from these women who have the strength and conviction to be able to face their oppressors without fear and with their pride intact.

PUBLISHED BY THE STUC WOMEN'S COMMITTEE

23

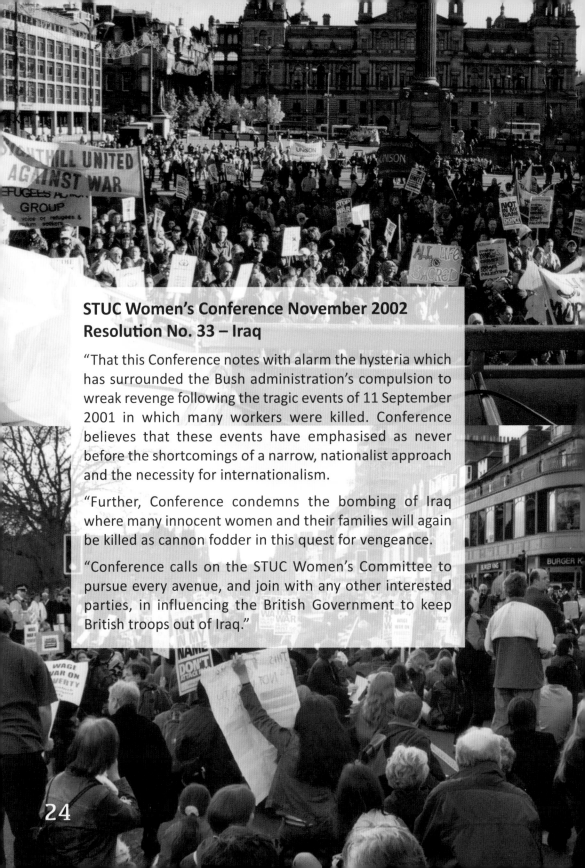

STUC Women's Conference November 2002
Resolution No. 33 – Iraq

"That this Conference notes with alarm the hysteria which has surrounded the Bush administration's compulsion to wreak revenge following the tragic events of 11 September 2001 in which many workers were killed. Conference believes that these events have emphasised as never before the shortcomings of a narrow, nationalist approach and the necessity for internationalism.

"Further, Conference condemns the bombing of Iraq where many innocent women and their families will again be killed as cannon fodder in this quest for vengeance.

"Conference calls on the STUC Women's Committee to pursue every avenue, and join with any other interested parties, in influencing the British Government to keep British troops out of Iraq."

The STUC has always concerned itself with economic and social policy matters, combining speaking up for employment rights with wider commitments to tackle racism, discrimination and all injustice. For a number of years, the STUC has taken the Saturday nearest to St. Andrew's Day (30 November) to hold a march and rally in Glasgow, to celebrate diversity and speak out against racism and inequality.

Campaigns against deportations and the harsh treatment of children and women by the UK Borders Agency and immigration services have been a priority for the STUC Women's Committee.

International Women's Day

International Women's Day (8 March) is a global day celebrating the economic, political and social achievements of women past, present and future. In some places like China, Russia, Vietnam and Bulgaria, International Women's Day is a national holiday. International Women's Day has its roots in the struggles of working women. In 1908, 15,000 women marched through New York City demanding shorter hours, better pay and voting rights. In 1910 at the second International Conference of Working Women in Copenhagen, Clara Zetkin (Leader of the "Women's Office" for the Social Democratic Party in Germany) proposed that every year in every country there should be a celebration on the same day - a Women's Day - to press for their demands. The Conference of over 100 women from 17 countries, representing unions, socialist parties, working women's clubs, greeted Zetkin's suggestion with unanimous approval and International Women's Day was the result.

In 1911, International Women's Day (IWD) was marked in a number of European countries on 19 March. More than one million women and men attended IWD rallies campaigning for women's rights to work, vote, be trained, to hold public office and end discrimination. In New York later that month, over 140 working women, mainly immigrants, lost their lives in a serious fire. This highlighted the terrible working conditions and the absence of any protective employment legislation, and International Women's Day subsequently provided a focus for women organising for justice and equality at work, as well as in wider society. By 1913, international discussions had agreed on the date of 8 March for International Women's Day, and it has been celebrated on this date each year worldwide since then.

1975 was designated as "International Women's Year" by the United Nations. In 2013, the United Nations theme for International Women's Day was "A promise is a promise: Time for action to end violence against women". In March 2013, The European TUC published research confirming the significant and disproportionate negative impact that the economic recession is having on women's employment.

ETUC Statement for International Women's Day 2013: Women are paying too high a price! Europe must break with austerity and deliver on equality

On 8 March 2013, International Women's Day (IWD), women worldwide will unite in solidarity to celebrate their courage, determination, and strength and to repeat their collective demand for a basic yet fundamental right: equality between women and men. The European Trade Union Confederation (ETUC) celebrates with them and salutes the contributions and achievements, large and small, of the millions of trade union women and men who are constantly striving for women's rights in and out of the workplace.

The STUC Women's Committee highlighted this too, focusing also on the increased pressure on women's health as a result of changes in the workplace. Using social media for the first time, the STUC Women's Committee campaign called for women to join a trade union. The message reached thousands of people worldwide as "TUC Global" and others passed it on through Twitter, bringing a truly international spirit to the trade union women who were handing out the same leaflets at railway stations in central Scotland.

EQUAL PAY

The conditions of women workers in Scotland came to the STUC attention from early on, in particular in the textile industry and with strong voices coming from Dundee. A clothing trades delegate, speaking at the 1909 STUC Congress in Dunfermline, warned of "the growing tendency of employers in all trades to substitute underpaid women labour for men's labour". A resolution calling for equal pay for equal work, and urging women workers to organise, was carried.

Scotland saw a number of equal pay strikes during World War II. Agnes McLean was the daughter of a Red Clydesider. She attended Socialist Sunday School and joined the union aged 15, leading an equal pay strike at the Rolls Royce factory in Hillington in 1943. The strike saw thousands of workers on strike for several days, before the women inspectors won their equal pay fight. Agnes went on to become a prominent activist for women workers' rights in the AEU and in the wider trade union movement.

Rolls Royce workers, Agnes McLean second from left.

The 1968 strike by female sewing machinists at the Ford factory in Dagenham is widely seen as the catalyst to the passing of the Equal Pay Act in 1970, for which the then Secretary of State for Employment, Barbara Castle MP, must also be given recognition. In fact, the struggle for equal pay goes right back to the earliest days of women organising in the workplace and in the labour movement. The STUC Women's Committee has continued to highlight the barriers to achieving equal pay.

STUC Women's Conference 2000

"Conference believes that equalities issues, including equal pay, must form an integral part of the STUC's overall economic agenda. It is now time for concerted action to win equal pay for the many thousands of women who deserve a decent wage, comparable to the wages men can expect to earn."

The Women's Conference in 2000 also highlighted the importance of the Care Sector, calling on the STUC to:
- negotiate and campaign to address the pay deficiency in this sector,
- value the work done by carers,
- increase the status of carers by negotiating for improved training,
- ensure the highest standards and levels of quality care.

SUPPORT THE LAIRD-PORTCH / JAEGER EQUAL PAY STRIKE

The equal Pay strike at the Laird-Portch factory in East Kilbride is now entering its sixth week. 450 workers, mainly women, came out after management repeatedly broke promises to close the enormous gap between unskilled men and skilled women — between £8 and £10 per week.

Laird-Portch is part og the giant Coats Paton multinational, with over 200 subsidiareis including Jaeger and Country Casuals. This week they announced they had trebled their profits and were applying to the government to lift restrictions so they can pay their shareholders more. Their profit comes from cheap female labour: this is why they are refusing equal pay, in an industry which employs 90% women

We ask for your help in publicising and assisting the strike in the following ways:

*help the pickets on Jaegers and Country Casuals. Dont shop there. Join the pickets for an hour on Saturdays.

*Come to the public meetings on Thursday June 9th and on Thursday June 16th to hear the strikers' case and express your support.

*Take copies of the collection sheet to raise money in your branch/ workplace.

Financial donations, messages of support to:
E. Nicklin (convenor)
Further informati on from E. Oldham, c/o women's centre

L A I R D - P O R T C H / J A E G E R   S T R I K E : A P P E A L

Now in its third week, this strike involving 450 members of the National Union of Tailors and Garment Workers arose out of a string of broken management promises about closing the enormous gap between skilled women's rates of pay and that of the lowest unskilled male rate.

Discussions with the multinational Coats — Paton group date back to January 1975 and throughout this period management have repeatedly failed to live up to agreements on how the gap was to be closed. The Company finally backed out of its last agreement to resolve the dispute through a job evaluation, and now maintains that a gap of over £10 per week between skilled women's rates and the lowest unskilled male rate is justified . The two Jaeger factories at Kilmarnock, and the warehouse staff at Jaeger, Alloa, have come out in support, and work is being blacked at the company's Ladybird plants.

Financial support is urgently required to maintain the strike and its 24-hour picket of the company plants. All donations to:

STRIKE COMMITTEE, NATIONAL UNION OF TAILORS AND GARMENT WORKERS, 534 SAUCHIEHALL STREET, GLASGOW

EQUAL PAY FOR WORK OF EQUAL VALUE — NOW!

ORGANISATION ....

NAME	AMOUNT	NAME	AMOUNT

In April 1977, women workers from the Laird Portch clothing factory in East Kilbride walked out for six weeks in a dispute over equal pay, demanding parity with unskilled male workers. Support grew with workers from the Kilmarnock Jaeger plant also walking out. The multinational Coates Paton eventually agreed to re-examine the grading structure in their UK factories. The clothing industry was feeling the consequences of the new 1976 Equal Pay Act.

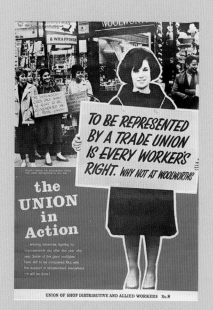

Woolworth strike, 1962

Women. Men. Different. Equal.
Equal Opportunities Commission Scotland

Did you know...

- Before 1975 a man could not be a midwife and that some Health Authorities refused to train married women as midwives.

- Before 1975 women had to leave the foreign office when they married.

- Before 1975 most married women could only get credit if a man guaranteed their loan.

- Before 1975 girls were not allowed to play rugby or football at school and women were not even allowed to play in official darts games.

- Before 1975 many schools taught different subjects to boys and girls.

LEE JEANS SIT-IN

In February 1981, a seven month long sit-in began at the American owned Lee Jeans factory in Greenock. The 240 workforce were first notified on 29 January 1981 that the factory would close with 90 days notice being given. The news came as a complete shock to the workforce, as valuable machinery had been installed the previous year, they had high production levels and industrial relations were good.

The trade union put forward a plan for work sharing until trade picked up. However, the company confirmed the closure the following week. A mass meeting was held in the canteen and the workforce overwhelmingly agreed that redundancy payments were no substitute for jobs.

As they believed they would be locked out if they left the factory that night, a vote was taken and the sit-in began. Many of the women employed in the Greenock factory were under the age of 25 and were the sole breadwinners of their households. Jobs were at a premium during a time of severe economic recession.

Women played a central role in this dispute, speaking at public meetings to argue their case. The STUC Women's Committee met with the Lee Jeans workers at the factory and encouraged other trade unionists to support the sit-in financially and politically. At STUC 1981 Congress, the following emergency motion was carried unanimously:

"That this Congress recognises the important roles being played by the workers of Lee Jeans in their magnificent struggle against closure of the factory. Congress calls on the General Council to request an immediate meeting with the Secretary of State for Scotland to deal with this urgent situation, as a first step, followed by any other positive action required to protect those workers."

A management buy-out in August 1981 secured jobs until unfortunately the factory went into receivership in 1983.

The Lee Jeans sit-in was an inspiration to women workers all over the world.

THE MINERS' STRIKE
ONE YEAR 1984 -1985

Emergency motion adopted at April 1984 STUC Congress
"That this Congress, recognising the serious situation facing the nation, arising from the dispute between the National Coal Board and the National Union of Mineworkers, declares the need for this Congress to support the miners in their struggle against pit and associated closures which will lead to severe job losses affecting other sections of industry – rail, steel, manufacturing and transport on land and sea.

"Congress, recognising the effect of the Coal Board plans on the Scottish economy, calls upon all affiliates to unite in support of the NUM in their present struggle to defend the Scottish economy as an important part of the general aim of Congress to end the scourge of mass unemployment.

"Congress therefore calls upon the movement to rally behind the miners with support in financial terms but also calls on the whole labour and trade union movement for various forms of action throughout Scotland in support of the miners and that an all-Scottish day of action be supported by Congress."

The Coal industry in the UK had been nationalised in 1947. The Conservatives won the 1979 General Election. Their government, headed up by Prime Minister, Margaret Thatcher, set about restructuring the industry, and curbing the power of the unions. Unachievable targets were set for the National Coal Board, and a programme of pit closures began. A number of pits in Scotland had been closed by the end of 1983. Early in 1984, with a further round of closures announced across the UK and local industrial action taking place, the National Union of Mineworkers called a national strike. By 14 March 1984, the industry was at a standstill.

NATIONAL UNION OF MINEWORKERS

COAL NOT DOLE

Norman Buchan MP, Mick McGahey, President of the Scottish Miners, and Margaret Wegg, Cardowan Women's Support Group

Throughout the centuries, women have been involved in struggle and none more poignant or needed as during the miners' strike in the nineteen eighties.

One of the first meetings for women in the Scottish coalfields, organised by the Scottish NUM Women's Support Group, was held at Lochgelly, Fife. The main speakers were Judith Hart MP and Jane McKay. The most memorable part of the event was the number of women from the mining communities who lined up to come to the rostrum to speak of their struggle.

Women from mining families knew the strike was more than defending the jobs of their partners, sons, brothers, uncles and fathers. Women recognised the struggle was not only to keep pits open and ensure there was a viable mining industry, it was also to defend their families and their communities.

Women and families were plunged into real poverty and women responded by establishing Women's Support Groups, who worked in strike centre kitchens and joined picket lines. Through women speaking at rallies, they galvanised support from thousands of individual people, to large and small organisations throughout Scotland. They knew the importance of forging links with women from trade unions, political parties, churches, women's groups and many other organisations. Another crucial meeting held at Dunfermline, organised by the Scottish NUM Women's Support Group, brought together representatives from all political parties (bar the Conservatives), the churches and trade unions, including the STUC Women's Committee. It was to this meeting that women from all over Scotland brought black bin bags full of basic necessities for women which they had collected at churches, trade union meetings and workplaces. The necessities included sanitary towels, tampax, knickers of all sizes, tights, soap, shampoos and even bottles of perfume. It was a wonderful women's event – Sisterhood at its best!

The Women's Support Group organised many, many meetings, none so frightening as the one held on 14 February, a date selected to demonstrate the caring loving attitude of women. A peaceful picket at Polkemmet Colliery, which had been flooded during the strike, saw women being confronted by a mass police presence, but the sisterhood and support these women gave each other made this peaceful protest all the more poignant. Women from the mining communities helped to tell the human story of the miners' struggle in Thatcher's Britain, and many of these women, politicised through their own struggles, became involved in local and national campaigns supporting local services, jobs, the NHS and the welfare state.

Support had come for the miners from every corner of Scotland, from towns and villages across the UK, and from all around the world. But the Government was also determined, using every means at its disposal to attack the NUM and through that, the wider trade union movement. Changes were made to the benefit system to deny support to children and families of striking miners. The destruction of the production capacity of the coal industry was a price the Government was willing to pay. Miners and their communities faced mounting debts.

36

On 4 March 1985, the union ended the strike, with an organised return to work. Polkemmet, Frances, Comrie, Killoch the list of pit closures went on from 1985. The industry was privatised in 1994, and by 2002 all Scottish mines had closed. A number of miners were sacked at the end of the strike, and campaigns were launched to support those victimised for fighting to save jobs and the industry.

Victimisation of Miners - statement from April 1985 STUC Congress

"That this Congress places on record its appreciation of the heroic struggle of Britain's miners, their families and communities in defence of jobs and the protection of Britain's energy requirements. Arising from that 12 months' struggle, Congress condemns the vindictive attitude of the N.C.B. in victimising over 200 Scottish miners for the 'crime' of defending their jobs."

Equal Voice

ISSUE 93/2

Women the losers in Tory Britain

by MAUREEN ROONEY

THE dispute at Timex is one of a series of industrial actions which have been bitterly contested, in the main by women. Today what is noticeable is the number of disputes in which the majority of participants are women, far removed from the traditional image of the striking worker.

It is not just the case that women have become more militant. The hard reality is that in Tory Britain women have in the main been the losers. Changing working practices, reduction in working conditions and benefits and the reduction of union power have all been part of the hallmark of Conservative Governments since 1979. Margaret Thatcher used to boast that she had broken the power of the unions, not only did she do that, she put women's rights back by years. 14 years on women still do not receive equal pay, women still make up the majority of the part-time workforce and women are still the ones predominantly protected by the Wages Councils.

Legacy of Tory rule

Already this year the female-dominated teachers' unions caused problems for the Government with their boycott of school tests. What is clear in many of these cases is the Government's apparent reluctance to follow anything other than an extreme line.

The Timex workers confronted a management who clearly thought that in 1990s Britain they could get away with sacking the whole workforce and in that dispute there were no winners, only losers. That is the legacy that 14 years of Conservative rule has left us.

Figures show that women still earn on average 70% of a man's wage, this is despite the fact that the Equal Pay Act is over 15 years old. Thus the majority of women still earn less than men and work in low-paid jobs. This is coupled with the increasing trend towards part-time work, which for women is a particularly worrying trend. 82% of all part-time workers are women who are therefore excluded from even the most basic of employment protection.

Political spite

The latest offering from the Government on the issue of industrial relations is the Employment Rights and Trade Union Reform Bill, soon to become law. This piece of legislation is viewed by many both inside and outside the labour movement as an act of pure political spite and having little or nothing to do with improving industrial relations. One of the Bill's central points is the removal of the Wages Councils and the limited protection that they afforded workers, who in the main were women. The Gov-

MAUREEN ROONEY

ernment's attitude at the time was that women who worked in sectors covered by the wages councils were working for pin money. Clearly the Government has completely lost touch with the reality of working women in 1990s Britain.

Anti-worker attitude

Britain's reluctance to sign up to the Social Chapter, their challenge to the Working Hours Directive and their failure to bring maternity leave into line with the best practices in Europe are all indicative of how they view the British worker. When the Government of the day has this kind of anti-worker attitude it is hardly surprising

that employers feel that they have the right to withdraw basic rights at any time they like. Timex is one good example, but another is the women formally employed at Burnsall Ltd., who continue to picket the site. There the striking employees claim that they were earning £30 a week less than the men, received no sick pay and worked a compulsory 65 hour week. As with the situation at Timex, Burnsall was in an area of high unemployment where replacement workers were easy to find.

Let us hope that both employers and the Government learn the lessons from Timex.

PUBLISHED BY THE STUC WOMEN'S COMMITTEE

Timex

In this painting, the overalls hanging on the line from inside the factory gate symbolised the actions of the Timex women. When learning they were sacked, they took their overalls off and threw them up in the air, some landing on the trees.

"In response to the Management's proposal in January 1993 to lay off over a hundred workers, the entire workforce withdrew their labour. The management responded by sacking all 343 workers (mainly women). Other women were employed to replace the sacked workforce. They crossed the picket line, bussed in by the Timex Managing Director, Peter Hall. The strike breakers accepted lower wages than the sacked workers had been paid.

It is with pride I look back and recall the friendship and sisterhood among the women during the dispute. Women who had never spoken in public were addressing meetings throughout Scotland, as well as taking their turn on the picket line. They were fighting for their livelihood and, like me, had worked in Timex since they were young lasses. They were astonishing - standing up for what they believed in. Yes, the management got what they wanted – the closure of Timex in Dundee. But for those of us who stood on the right side of the picket line at Timex, we can hold our heads high in our city."

Sandra Walker, a former assembly line worker at Timex (an AEU member who also served on the STUC Women's Committee) speaking March 2013.

I joined the Union because

I knew that a strong union membership strengthened the power of the union to challenge the changes brought in by the employer.

I joined the union because I believe that a collective voice is louder and stronger than an individual.

I felt I could obtain professional & non-biased advice from the union. Being in the union would make me feel part of an organisation which shares similar beliefs and values.

there was no alternative, the unity of the union was the only weapon we had in our fight against oppression in the workplace.

A Woman's Right to Choose

The right to decide what happens to our bodies; to be able to control our own fertility and to have access to free contraception and abortion are central to the demands for women's emancipation. Prior to the 1967 Abortion Act, it was estimated that up to 100,000 illegal abortions were being carried out in Britain every year. In 1966 alone, 40 women died as a result of having to resort to dangerous methods. David Steel's historic 1967 legislation did not provide abortion on demand, but it did allow for any woman who needed an abortion, with the backing of two doctors, that right. Attacks on the legislation have included James White MP in 1975, William Benyon MP in 1977, John Corrie MP in 1979, and the Alton Bill 1988. The trade union movement, responding to women's demands, played a leading role from 1979. The TUC organised 80,000 in London to protest against Corrie, with many trade unionists travelling from Scotland. The biggest demonstration ever in Britain in support of women's rights was acknowledged at the 1980 STUC Congress.

At the STUC Congress in 1980 the following composite motion was debated:

"That this Congress commends the General Council and the Women's Advisory Committee for their consistent support and initiatives in defence and extension of abortion rights, and particularly welcomes the unity between trade union and women's movements achieved in this campaign.

Congress believes that restrictions upon free legal and safe abortion constitutes a fundamental attack upon women's rights and upon the health and welfare standards of working people.

Congress therefore, pledges its continuing act of support to all those who campaign and act to ensure wider access to contraceptive education and against any attempts to restrict or amend the 1967 Abortion Act. Congress further supports affiliated unions campaigning to protect and improve the outpatient abortion clinics provided for under the National Health Service.

Congress considers that in sponsoring mass demonstrations against restrictive legislation, the TUC and STUC have set a magnificent example to the International Labour Movement and resolves by all means and at all levels to extend the unity and action thus forged in the fight for women's rights."

Glasgow, Saturday 16th January 1988, demonstration called
by FAB (Fight the Alton Bill) and STUC

"Building the Alton Bill demonstration gave me a chance to talk
about the 1967 Abortion Act in my union branch. The support
I got was fantastic. They gave money and agreed to support the
the demonstration. I will never forget how proud I was to walk
behind my trade union banner that day and to see many, many
more union banners supporting women's rights."

"Jo Richardson MP, Labour's Shadow Minister for Women, was leading the fight against the Alton Bill in Parliament. As I sat beside her on the platform, looking at the huge crowd, I thought, how inspiring it is for both of us that so many women were throwing themselves into the campaign. It's giving us strength."

Maria Fyfe, Labour Member of Parliament for Glasgow Maryhill 1987 to 2001

"The hall was full with women all wanting to make their voices heard on this difficult but important issue, it was so heartening. The STUC Women's Committee had played a leading role in the organisation of the Fight Alton Bill campaign in Scotland."

Yvonne Strachan, TGWU Scotland Women's Organiser and a member of the STUC Women's Committee

Equal Voice

SPRING 1988   PRICE 20p

Fight Alton's Bill

DAVID ALTON'S Abortion (Amendment) Bill received its second reading in the House of Commons on 22 January by a majority of only 45 votes. The Bill seeks to introduce a time limit for abortion at the beginning of the 18th week of pregnancy. It is seen as one of the most serious attacks on women's rights in many years and has been overwhelmingly opposed by STUC and TUC women's conferences.

Who voted for Alton?

Alton was supported not only by those MPs who think that an 18 week limit is justified, but also by a number of MPs — from all parties — who hoped that the Bill would be amended at Committee stage to 24 weeks, with certain exceptions being made. In Scotland, 22 MPs voted for Alton, with 13 abstaining or recording no vote.

The next step

The Bill will now be considered by a Select Committee of the House of Commons. It will sit every Wednesday from March 16th onwards, and should come back to the House for its report stage and Third Reading on one of the five Fridays set aside for Private Members' Bills between April and May.

Amendments can be made at Committee. Although Alton has indicated that he is not prepared to change the 18 week limit, he might consider two possible amendments in an attempt to retain the votes of some MPs who supported him, with reservations, at the Second Reading. These might be: a) for women whose babies are likely to be born with particular disabilities, and b) for women who have been raped, and have reported to a police station!

However, there are bound to be time limit amendments, in particular for 24 weeks. The idea of 24 weeks needs to be closely considered.

In 1986 there were 29 abortions in the whole of Britain after 24 weeks. This includes *one* in Scotland. These 29 are the exceptions — the very difficult and most needy cases, for example.

- foetal abnormality where the results of screening are not known until 20-24 weeks
- young women too ignorant or afraid to come forward earlier
- menopausal women who thought they were too old to be pregnant
- rape victims
- women who are victims of the delays in the NHS or have been misdiagnosed
- foreign women — including Irish and Scottish women — who are denied abortion facilities in their own country

And of course, a 24 week limit in Law would mean a 20/22 week limit in practice, as doctors leave a 2—4 week margin of error in calculating dates.

Scotland has no time limits, and Scotland's Common Law position is considered better, as it allows for flexibility. A 24 week limit would mean legislating AGAINST the exceptions.

Positive contributions to the Committee Stage

Among the Committee are two Scottish MPs who voted

A packed Glasgow City Halls for January's Scottish Alton Bill Rally
(Photo: Alan Wylie)

against the Bill: Frank Doran (Labour, Aberdeen South) and Lewis Moonie (Labour, Kirkcaldy). Frank Doran has said that there could be an opportunity (however slim) to debate ideas of making the '67 Abortion Act better, and therefore reduce the number of late abortions, such as:

- provision of direct access to NHS clinics up to 12 weeks on request
- provision of quality professional counselling
- obligations on Health Boards to provide abortion facilities locally
- provision of the right of appeal in the system (at present, if refused abortion, there is no right of appeal against the decision)
- the streamlining of referral practices to overcome unnecessary delays.

If you have any ideas to make the '67 Act better and thereby reduce the number of late abortions, let us know!

Action needed now!

Continue to write to your MP and visit his/her surgery

MPs who voted against Alton should be congratulated, and urged to give continued support:

MPs who did not vote should be asked why, and arguments for a 'NO' vote next time:

MPs who voted for Alton should be made aware of your anger, and urged through argument to change their vote at Third Reading. Labour MPs should be reminded of Party policy to defend the '67 Act, and their responsibility to defend women's rights:

MPs who voted hoping for a 24 week limit need to be convinced of the dangers of this position, and that the only option at a Third Reading must be outright rejection of the Bill. Any reduction in the time limits will bring suffering to thousands of women and their families.

A vote against Alton is a vote for women and choice!

PUBLISHED BY THE STUC WOMEN'S COMMITTEE

1980's

Women continue to organise together for equality and abortion rights through conferences, debates, and demonstrations. Social media is now used widely too, but has not replaced the handmade banners and placards that are still to be seen on the streets, campaigning for a woman's right to choose.

1990's

2000's

2012

46

To the Rt Honourable George Younger M.P.
and Secretary of State for Scotland
Women Trade Unionists in Scotland today do not
want to see their standard of living eroded and
opportunities for work lessened. Unfortunately
this is increasingly the case.
We believe Government policies, aligned to their
pursuit of values prevalent in Victorian times, sorely
undermine established rights which women have
rightly demanded and actively fought for.
• We want a Health Service free at the time of need,
but the Government favours Privatisation and
commercial Medical Care --------------------------
• We want the best education for our Children,
but the Government provides less and less to finance
Scottish Local Authorities to enable improvements
in the Compulsory sector, let alone in Nursery
facilities for the Under Fives
• We want an effective and caring social service
system but the Government demanded Cuts which mean
less trained and Caring Staff to look after the
Elderly, Sick and Disabled ~~~~~~~~~~~~~~~~~
• We want the right to Work but the
Government has created an economic climate
whereby over a hundred thousand women in Scotland
are looking for Work, with little or no prospect
of ever securing Employment ~~~~~~~~~~~~~~~
The Government has tried to turn the clock back.
But Women Trade Unionists in the 80's like their
Sisters throughout this country, will not turn
their backs on the Daughters of Tomorrow.
The General Council of the Scottish T.U.C.
and its Women's Advisory Committee have
consistently asked you and the Government
to abandon economic theories which do not work.
We are now demanding not asking that
you do not abandon the Women of Scotland

From 1979, the policies of Margaret Thatcher's Conservative Government created a severe recession. The STUC Women's Committee campaigned against the increasing inequality and poverty facing women. In 1987, working on the theme of "no return to Victorian values", a delegation, suitably attired in Victorian costume, presented a petition to the then Secretary of State for Scotland, George Younger MP.

POLL TAX

The Conservative Government at Westminster chose Scotland to trial a new form of local taxation in 1989. The "Community Charge", which became known as the Poll Tax, meant that all adults were to pay the same tax per person, irrespective of income or property. This was manifestly unfair, and rapidly led to non-payment campaigns, demonstrations, and massive arrears building up for local authorities. The STUC was at the heart of the All-Scotland Anti Poll Tax campaign. The mass campaign spread to England and Wales with the introduction of the Poll Tax in 1990. By 1992, Scottish councils were facing over £312 million in arrears, the Tax was clearly unworkable, and the Government was defeated.

Poll Tax

"That this Conference expresses total opposition to the proposed Poll Tax, as unfair, unworkable and uncollectable.

"Conference further condemns the proposed uniformed business rate as breaking the direct link between local businesses and local authority. A nationally set business rate will make it more difficult for local authorities to maintain jobs and services.

"If introduced, those hardest hit will include:

1) women who have the major responsibility for managing household finances;

2) young people who will be faced for the first time with finding substantial additional funds to pay the Poll Tax;

3) the ethnic communities, particularly those living in extended families;

4) senior citizens who will have to find 20% of the Poll Tax.

"Conference records its appreciation to the Poll Tax Steering Committee set up by the STUC for the work done to date on the Poll Tax.

"Conference recognises the key role that women have to play in the Poll Tax campaign. Women in the Labour Movement are the most effective campaigners in increasing the awareness of women of the impact of the Poll Tax on themselves and their families.

"The STUC Women's Committee should continue to liaise with the Scottish Labour Women's Committee to explore joint initiatives to involve more women in the campaign.

"Conference therefore calls on the Women's Committee to continue to support the Steering Committee, individual union campaigns, and to encourage participation in broad based Labour Movement and local initiatives against the Tax."

Poll Tax text is from the General Council Report 1989

1989 witnessed the STUC Women's Committee put in writing the foundation for gender equality and new politics in Scotland, submitting a comprehensive response to the Women's Issues Group of the Scottish Constitutional Convention. The STUC call was for a Scottish Parliament with family friendly hours, childcare arrangements available for members and staff of the Parliament, mainstreaming equal opportunities, openness and accountability and a new politics, which would help improve the lives of women, men and children in Scotland.

Its most radical proposal, however, was for equal numbers of women and men as elected representatives. Thus, the 50/50 Campaign emerged as the most significant principle of fairness, justice and equality in the devolution debate.

Of prime importance was to have the support of the trade union movement. A debt of gratitude is owed to those trade union women who first raised the idea of gender representation in the Scottish Parliament within their own unions. Without the backing of trade unions, that key principle would have been dead in the water. The Women's Committee created the Women's Co-ordination Group, with a range of women's organisations, with women in political parties, with academics, politicians, and many others to win support for its 50/50 Campaign. Informal discussions with Labour, Scottish Liberal Democrats and Scottish National Party women examined strategies to win support for equal representation of women and men in the Scottish Parliament. These were an essential part of the Campaign and the women from the political parties all played a significant role in informing their own party's views on women's representation in the Parliament.

It was a compelling Campaign, which ignited a deep sense of natural justice and fairness for a society based on equality. The lead taken by women in this campaign helped to ensure that Scottish Labour and Scottish Liberal Democrats agreed an Electoral Pact in November 1995 to operate a specific mechanism to achieve gender balance in a Scottish Parliament. In 1999, 37% of elected members of the first Scottish Parliament were women. Scotland had one of the highest numbers of women in any legislative chamber in the world, and equal opportunities had been adopted as one of the key principles of that Parliament.

Initiatives such as placing an advert in national newspapers supporting the 50/50 campaign, was a part of the work on the women's coordination group.

Appeal for 50/50: Equal Representation of Women and Men

The establishment of a Scottish Parliament will provide a unique opportunity to change the representation and participation of all Scotland's people. It is crucial, in the name of justice, fairness and equality, that women are able to play a full and equal part in the new Scottish Parliament.

We support the proposal that there should be a constitutional obligation on political parties to ensure gender balance in Scotland's Parliament — right from its beginning!

Marie Allan, Donald Anderson, Janet Andrews, John and Carwyn Anzani, Anne Begg, Marjorie Bell, Rhona Brankin, Esther Breitenbach, Margaret Bryce-Stafford, Ivy Cameron, N. Cameron, Jane Campbell, Audrey Canning, Eric Canning, May Carlin, Eileen Carmichael, Kay Carmichael, Jane Carolan, Willie Carolan, Dougie Chalmers, A. Chisholm, Malcolm Chisholm, Campbell Christie, Alex Clark, Barbara Clark, Michael Connarty, Rev. Helen Cook, Nancy Coull, Prof. Bernard Crick, Anne Currie, Graham Dane, Gina Davidson, Ian Davidson, Janet Davidson, Kath Davies, Alison Gean Davis, Christine Davis, Mary Fitch Deans, Democratic Left, Jim Devine, Mary Donnelly, David Donnison, Bob Dow, David Drever, Dundee Trades Council, Jude Dunn, Educational Institute of Scotland, Liz Elkind, Bonnie Dudley Edwards, Owen Dudley Edwards, Ella Egan, Engender, Alex Falconer, Falkirk & District Trades Council, Kathie Finn, Maria Fyfe, Jane George, Joan Gibson, Sheila Gilmore, Glasgow District Trades Council, Glasgow Maryhill CLP, Marlyn Glen, GMB: Scottish Regional Committee, Norman Godman, Louise Goldsack, Mary Gordon, Archie Graham, Juliet Grant-Hutchison, Joyce Gray, Nigel Griffiths, Edith Hamilton, Hampden Advertising, Mary Harrison, Meg Heggie, Marion Hersh, Anne Hepburn, Leslie Hills, Norma Hurley, Helen Hood (President, YWCA Scottish National Council), Margaret Jamieson, Aileen Johnston, Jack Jones, Helen Kay, Mike Kirby, Irene Kitson, Beverley Klein, Fiona Knowles, Sonia Kordiak, Gillian Kulwicki, Rose Lambie, Johann Lamont, Richard Leonard, Helen Liddell, Deborah Lincoln, Isobel Lindsay, Sheelagh Lister, Barbara Littlewood, George MacBride, Charles McCafferty, Margaret McCafferty, Angela McCallum, Cathleen McCarron, Pat McCarron, Ingrid McClements, Rosina McCrae, Moira McCrossan, Margery Palmer McCulloch, Morag MacDonald, Ronnie McDonald, Anne McGuire, Ailsa Macintosh, Ann Macintosh, Farquhar Macintosh, Margaret Macintosh, Alec McKay, F. MacKay, Ian McKay, Jane McKay, Mairi McKay, Willie McKelvey, Elinor Mckenzie, Gordon Mackenzie, Catherine McLagan, Patricia McLaren, Anne MacLean, Stewart MacLennan, Walter MacLellan, Daphne McNab, Ruth Madigan, Sheila Maher, Deborah Marsden, Kathleen Marshall, Jim Martin, John Maxton, Anne Middleton, Ian Millar, Tommy Morrison, Marion Morton, Peter Morton, MSF Regional Council Women's Committee, Muir Society of Labour and Radical Lawyers, Jean Muir, June Murray, Tom Nairn, Margaret Nicol, NUCPS Women Delegates to 1994 Women's Conference, NUM: Scotland Area, Janis Paulin, J. R. Payne, Mary Picken, Richard Pietrasik, Van Pietrasik, Rose Pipes, Queen's Park/Crosshill Labour Party, Marion Ralls, Sandra Ramsay, Veronica Rankin, Sheena Rennie, Penny Richardson, Ernie Ross, Alan Scott, Scottish Education for Action and Development, Scottish Health Visitors' Association, Scottish Joint Action Group, Scottish Labour Women's Committee, Scottish Labour Women's Caucus, Scottish Women's Action Network, Linda Shanahan, Mary Shanahan, Roona Simpson, Gerry Skelton, Alex Smith, Charlotte Smith, Grahame Smith, Mary Smith, Matt & Eileen Smith, Bill Speirs, Rachel Squire, Helen Stevens, Mhairi Stewart, Yvonne Strachan, Audrey Strain, Elizabeth Stow, Strathclyde Labour Group, Pat Stuart, Lesley Sutherland, Lynn Tett, TGWU Ayrshire District Committee, TGWU Borders District Committee, TGWU Borders Women's Committee, TGWU Dumfries District Committee, TGWU Dundee District Committee, TGWU Dundee Women's Advisory Committee, TGWU Galashiels 7/117 Branch, TGWU Scottish Regional Committee, TGWU Scottish Women's Advisory Committee, Carol Thomson, Gillian Thomson, Alison Thornton, UNISON Scotland, Maryanne Ure, Louise Walker, Lorraine Watson, Mike Watson, N. A. Watson, Tracey White, Paul Williamson, Ruth Winters, Alison M. Winton, Eric Young, G. Young, Diana Holland

50 50

Advert in Scotsman Friday 2nd December 1994

The STUC Women's Committee

50 / 50 Song

STRENGTHENING DEMOCRACY
50
50
WOMEN AND MEN

We're not afraid to go out in the open
For we know that our campaign is right
So we're stating our case plain and simple
And to get it we'll put up a fight

CHORUS
One, two, three, four, tell the people what we're for ....
Yes, we're for 50 / 50, easy peasy, half for him and half for measy
Guarantees we'll be there on the day
50 / 50 power sharing, proves to us you're really caring
That Scottish women should now have their say

And so we'll take our campaign to the people
And united we'll make sure our power
Will give women their fare share of say so
And our Scottish democracy flower

CHORUS
One, two, three, four, tell the people what we're for ....
Yes, we're for 50 / 50, easy peasy, half for him and half for measy
Guarantees that we'll all have a choice
We make up the Scottish nation, more than half the population
So come on sisters, and let's hear your voice

One, two, three, four, tell the people what we're for ....
Yes, we're for 50 / 50, easy peasy, half for him and half for measy
Guarantees we'll be there on the day
50 / 50 power sharing, proves to us you're really caring
That Scottish women can now have their say

OHHHHHHHHHH YEHHHHHHHHHH !!!

Jean Harrison, (COHSE, former member STUC Women's Committee)

STUC Women's Agenda for the Scottish Parliament in May 1999

Having secured commitments that the new Parliament would be more representative of the society which it would be representing, the STUC Women's Committee turned its attention to campaigning on the policies that would improve women's lives in Scotland. The STUC Women's Agenda was prepared with a wide range of women's organisations, and presented to all the candidates in the 1999 Scottish Parliament elections, summing up priorities for the new Scotland.

It included demands for:

- Championing family-friendly policies, equal pay, and tackling bullying and harassment.
- Extending the provision of flexible, accessible and affordable childcare, which meets the real needs of working parents.
- Embracing the principles of lifelong learning and funding lifelong learning initiatives, ensuring that adequate opportunities exist for working women to return to education.
- Ensuring women are properly represented within the Parliament itself at all levels in policy and decision making.
- Ensuring that future employment, economic development and skills strategies acknowledge and address fully the needs of women.

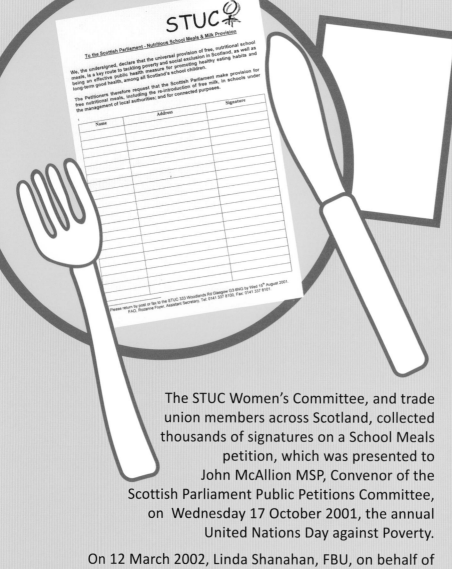

The STUC Women's Committee, and trade union members across Scotland, collected thousands of signatures on a School Meals petition, which was presented to John McAllion MSP, Convenor of the Scottish Parliament Public Petitions Committee, on Wednesday 17 October 2001, the annual United Nations Day against Poverty.

On 12 March 2002, Linda Shanahan, FBU, on behalf of the STUC Women's Committee, spoke at the Public Petitions Committee in the Parliament:

"This is a long-term strategy about building a Scotland that we and the generations after us will be proud of. The provision of universal, free nutritious school meals is not a solution in itself, but the beginning of a radical change in how we value our society."

This is an ongoing STUC Women's Committee Campaign.

51st STUC Women's Conference, City Chambers, Glasgow
22nd November 1978

Agenda

i) Address of Welcome.

ii) Chairman's Address.

iii) Amendment to the Constitution:

Delete—" 2. Date of Annual Conference.—The Conference shall meet annually in the month of November."

Insert—" 2. Date of Annual Conference.—The Conference shall meet annually, two consecutive days in November."

—Women's Advisory Committee.

iv) Consideration of Report of Committee.

v) Motions.

1. **Charter for the Under-Fives**

" That this Conference believes that only a comprehensive Charter for the under-fives will enable child care to receive the importance required to give the fullest benefits in nursery services, pre-nursery education and day care provision.

" To this end, we urge Conference to adopt the following Charter :—

* a national plan for under-fives services ;
* a massive expansion of education and day care places ;
* an end to low pay in the nursery service ;
* to restore cuts in nursery building ;
* under-fives facilities to be available on demand, free of charge ;
* to base the expansion of services on nursery centres ;
* to abolish the Nursery Nurses' Examination Board and create an integrated training scheme for all under-fives workers ;
* to provide pre-school facilities with flexible hours to meet the needs of working parents ;
* local councils to draw up a development plan for under-fives services ;
* to change the law on childminding and registration ;
* one Government Department to have responsibility for all under-fives services."

—National Union of Public Employees.

2. **The Under-Fives**

" That this Conference endorses the major recommendations of the T.U.C. Working Party Report 'The Under-Fives' and demands that the S.T.U.C. take immediate action to campaign for the implementation of these recommendations."

—Association of Cinematograph, Television and Allied Technicians.

Amendment to Motion No. 2

After the word " Conference " on the first line, insert :
" recognising that our economy cannot function wtihout women workers, believes that the State has a responsibility to provide nurseries. Conference consequently . . ."

After the word " recommendations " on the last line, insert :
" in order that places at nursery schools within the State education system are free of charge ".

—Amalgamated Union of Engineering Workers: Engineering Section.

4

Building on years of campaigning for good quality childcare, the 1978 STUC Women's Conference adopted a Charter for the Under Fives. The call for direct investment in the childcare workforce and infrastructure, and highlighting the economic and social benefits that universal childcare provision brings, was again at the top of the STUC Women's Conference agenda in 2012.

I joined the Union because

I knew that the best way to have your voice heard was through a union.

I joined when I started working here. I believed in the concept of unions but deep down I probably thought of them as representing groups of men doing physical jobs. But we had women as reps and speakers, and that made it seem more relevant to me

MY FATHER WAS A GREAT ADVOCATE OF UNIONS SO I WAS AWARE OF THEM FROM AN EARLY AGE. AS SOON AS I WAS ABLE TO I JOINED UP.
FOR ME IT'S A QUESTION OF FAIRNESS, MAKING SURE PEOPLE ARE TREATED FAIRLY AND NO-ONE SUFFERS JUST SO ANOTHER CAN MAKE A PROFIT.

I wanted to be part of the collective that represents the workers and gives them a voice!

Clause 28 and Section 2A were amendments brought forward by the Conservative Government in 1988, to local government legislation effective in England, Wales and Scotland. The effect was to place constraints on speaking about homosexuality within educational institutions, and in some areas had resulted in the closure of LGBT support groups for students, or restrictions on teachers and on classroom materials. Within the first year of the new Parliament in Scotland, the Scottish Government indicated its intentions to repeal the offending Clause. Despite a massive offensive campaign from those opposed to LGBT equality, it was repealed in Scotland on 21 June 2000, and subsequently in November 2003 in England and Wales.

Statement endorsed by STUC Congress April 2000

"The STUC has long worked to build a democratic Scotland, where all people are socially included and respected, regardless of their age, race, gender, disability, sexuality, religion or family situation, where every child in Scotland can expect their identity and their family ties to be respected and valued, where the true family values of love, respect, honesty, commitment and stability are promoted alongside tolerance and the celebration of our diversity.

"The General Council is, therefore, seeking support from affiliates to:

i) continue to do everything possible to support the Scottish Executive in its decision to repeal Section 28, and dispel the myths generated by the "Keep the Clause" Campaign;

ii) mobilise trade union members in Scotland to support the March for Equality and Diversity being organised to take place in Edinburgh on Saturday, 24 June; and

iii) examine the existing provisions by other countries of legislation prohibiting incitement to hatred, with a view to such legislation being considered by the Public Petitions Committee of the Scottish Parliament, in order that the persecution of minority groups can be outlawed in the future."

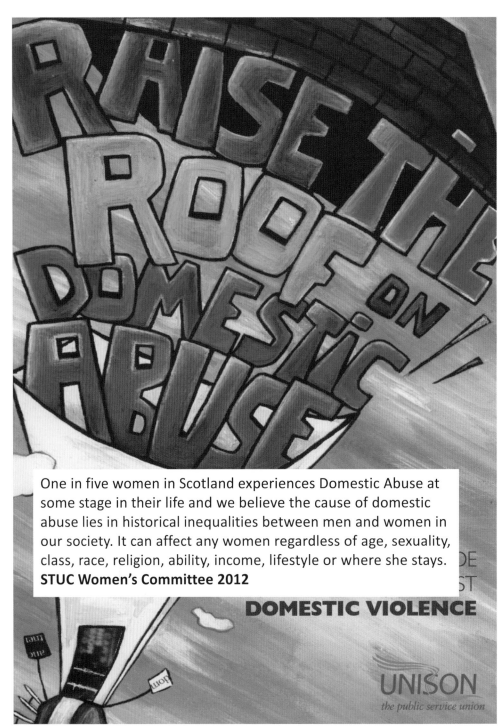

One in five women in Scotland experiences Domestic Abuse at some stage in their life and we believe the cause of domestic abuse lies in historical inequalities between men and women in our society. It can affect any women regardless of age, sexuality, class, race, religion, ability, income, lifestyle or where she stays.
STUC Women's Committee 2012

DOMESTIC VIOLENCE

UNISON
the public service union

Image from UNISON Campaign November 1999

Gude Cause

In October 2009, a march and celebration took place in Edinburgh to commemorate the 'Gude Cause' procession of 1909. The STUC was happy to lend its support. Women, men and young people from across Scotland came together to celebrate, but also to commit to continuing the fight for equality.

60

Health and safety legislation has brought some protection for workers over the years, and provisions for maternity and paternity leave have been improved. However, trade unions face a constant battle to ensure that rights are defended and good policies implemented. There are still many risks to health in the workplace, and the campaigns run by trade unions are crucial, as is strong representation.

NEWS RELEASE

November 5th 2010   For immediate release

Women Trade Union Leaders to Resist Senseless and Unjust Austerity Measures

60 women trade union leaders from across the UK and the Republic of Ireland have been meeting in Derry 4/5 November and believe that the austerity budgets being implemented in England, Wales, Scotland, Northern Ireland and the Republic of Ireland will not only affect women disproportionately, but will also be bad for the economy and our society.

Amongst those hardest hit will be lone parents. "Not only will women be worse off as a result of benefit cuts, but women are likely to also be the biggest losers when it comes to public sector pay freezes and jobs cuts", said Sarah Veale from the TUC.

In Wales, a recent poll showed that a majority of people feel that the cuts are being implemented unfairly. "42,000 public sector jobs are now at risk in Wales – 2/3 of public sector workers are women", said Julie Cook of the WTUC.

Elaine Dougall from the STUC said "A united trade union voice will lead the challenge to the government's short sighted austerity measures and promote an agenda that focuses on economic growth, the provision of jobs and services and equality for all."

Taryn Trainor, joint Chair of the ICTU Women's Committee, said "Of the £8 billion to be raised by the Budget changes in Northern Ireland, £5.8 billion will be paid by women. Women on low incomes will be forced to 'make do' with far less for their families. It must be resisted."

Joint Chair, Carol O'Brien, added: "It is critical that Budget decisions seek to alleviate the worst consequences of the recession on women by protecting the most vulnerable women and ensuring that progress that has been made towards equality for women is not reversed." She urged all to support the demonstration planned for Saturday, November 27 in Dublin.

ENDS

The UK elections in May 2010 returned a
Tory/Liberal Democrat coalition. From the outset
the Coalition made clear that working people
would pay for the financial crisis caused by the
banking collapse of 2008. One of the first big
labour movement demonstrations was called
by the STUC, and on 23 October 2010,
thousands marched in Edinburgh
to put forward an alternative.

On Saturday 26 March 2011, ½ million trade union members, and their families joined the TUC "March for the Alternative" in London. Protestors came from every corner of the country, workers from the private and public sector, from industry and from the voluntary sector. The STUC chartered two trains and many buses, and thousands of Scottish workers and their families travelled to London for the day. This was the largest mobilisation in the United Kingdom since the anti-Iraq war protests in 2003.

"The STUC represents over 300,000 trade union women in Scotland.

Increasingly, women are the majority in many of our affiliates, in some cases as much as 60-70%. The majority are low paid. Many are struggling under this Government's austerity programme, or let's call it what it really is - a direct attack on the poor, a protection racket for the rich and outright contempt for working people.

We are organising in response to this and we are giving women a voice."

Eileen Dinning, UNISON, Chair STUC Women's Committee.
Addressing the TUC Women's Conference, London, March 2013.

Pensions are under attack

The Tory led Coalition wants to make millions of people pay more, is threatening to make them work longer - and wants everyone to get a lot less at the end of it. Cutting public service workers' pensions won't make anyone's pension in the private sector better. In fact, it will make it harder for us to win pensions justice for all.

Workers in public services are modestly paid. Their pay has been frozen while the price of basics is shooting up. Now many are being told to accept major changes by a UK Government which happily cancelled the banker's bonus tax which could have raised 3 billion pounds. It's wrong to make workers in public services suffer to pay for bailing out the banks. The Tory-led Coalition is attacking pensions and the Scottish Government is doing little to stand in its way. That is why the STUC along with the TUC has called a day of action for pensions justice on 30 November.

STUC Campaign for Pensions Justice 2011

"Women's pensions are about financial independence and security."

"We need a regulated pensions industry that works for savers, not shareholders."

"We need a pension system that enables everyone to live with dignity in retirement."

"They said that public sector pensions were 'gold-plated' when The Hutton report, commissioned by the (UK) government, says that the median pension was £5,600 – that is, half of all public sector pensions are less than £5,600. This is hardly "gold-plated."

On 30 November 2011, more than two million public sector workers across the UK took strike action, with more than 20 trade unions joining together in a massive show of strength, defending the pensions of the workforce today, and arguing for fairness and investment in the future.

STUC Women's Committee November 2012

Front row:
Ann Henderson, Assistant Secretary/
Secretary to the STUC Women's Committee;
Natasha Gerson, Equity/STUC General Council;
Margaret Boyd, GMB; Elaine Dougall, Unite;
and Annie McCrae, EIS.
Second Row:
Joyce Stevenson, CWU;
Ann Farrell, Unite;
Agnes Tolmie, Unite/STUC General Council;
and Sharon Edwards, PCS.
Third Row:
Davena Rankin, UNISON;
Ann Joss, RMT;
Pauline Rourke, CWU/STUC General Council;
Annette Drylie, GMB;
Linda Delgado, Unite; and
Anne Dean, GMB.
Members not present:
Eileen Dinning, UNISON;
Tricia Donnelly, GTUC;
Susan Coutts, USDAW;
Heather Meldrum, Community/STUC General Council;
Lorna Binnie, Falkirk TUC;
and Margaret Anslow, TSSA.

STUC Centenary Women's Banners

The banner project was organised by the STUC Women's Committee as part of the 1997 celebrations to mark the Centenary of the Scottish Trades Union Congress. It involved women (and a few men) throughout Scotland in the creation of a series of five banners which document, commemorate and promote the activities of Scottish women in the trade union movement. The banners were first shown at the STUC Women's Conference in Dundee in November 1997. They offer a lasting and inspirational record of women's role in shaping the last century in Scotland. With guidance from the Women's Committee, research by Sarah Collier and designs by Clare Higney, and involving the artists Sally Thomson and Kate Downie, the banners were created by different groups.

Green Banner

"Women in the Community" captures women's positive action within the community from the stoicism of the War Years to the determination of the Zero Tolerance Campaign today. Hands curl round the unfolding lotus flower, the Buddhist symbol, representing our support for a multi-cultural Scotland. Made at the Arts project for Women in Aberdeen.

Red Banner

"Women for Freedom" promotes international solidarity. With the page open on the song of The Women's Internationale, a table of leaflets, books, pamphlets and badges records our connection with other women in the world. Made by women in Stirling at the Cowane Centre and The Smith Art Gallery and Museum.

Yellow Banner

"Women and Opportunity" highlights jobs, training and nursery provision. Different hands hold emblems of progress, such as a certificate for education, money, and a trade union membership card. Made in the Carnegie Library at Dunfermline

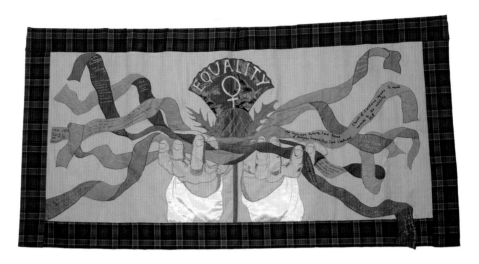

Purple Banner

"Women for Equality" focuses on suffrage, equal pay and anti-racism. 10 ribbons tell the story of women's progress decade by decade over the past one hundred years. Made by Glasgow's Community Banner Group at Washington Street Arts Centre.

Blue Banner

"Protecting the Future" depicts peace, environmental issues. As the leaves and acid rain fall, a dove soars into a sky embroidered with our hopes for the future. Made by Glasgow's Community Banner Group at Washington Street Arts Centre.

We so often hear reports of BME workers having problems in the workplace, where there is clearly an insidious racism at work, but too often we hear people say that they find it difficult to challenge, and difficult to convince others that racism is happening. I know that ethnic minority women are particularly suffering these attacks and it is simply unacceptable. We need unions who are ready to stand beside workers, and who understand the specific effect that racism and gender discrimination can have. That is why the work of the Black Workers' Committee and the Women's Committee is so vital.

STUC Black Workers' Committee
Chair, Nazerin Wardrop, UNITE

The STUC Youth Committee is organising a variety of events and using social media to network and reach a larger number of young trade unionists. It is vitally important that we engage with the new generation and deliver a good gender balance in activism. We continue to work with the STUC to promote unions into schools, colleges and youth groups. Our next campaign will be on zero hours contracts, and we are developing a charter for fair work experience.

STUC Youth Committee
Chair, Megan McCrossan, EIS

Conference, the STUC LGBT workers are starting to write their history into the weave of the fabric that makes us part of our strong and proud STUC. Sisters, on our marches and disputes take a look around, your LGBT colleagues will be there...not behind you, not ahead of you but standing alongside you. Together we will challenge all forms of justice and inequality whether they occur here or in other parts of the world. Our legacy is to inspire future activists to help others.

STUC Lesbian, Gay, Bisexual and Transgender Workers' Committee
Jenny Douglas, UNITE, at STUC Women's Conference 2012

Predictably, one of the main topics of discussion at our Conference this year was Welfare Reform. This affects women as disabled people, and as carers of disabled people. As a disabled woman, I am dismayed and disgusted at the attacks by this Coalition Government on our hard fought for rights, and their attempts to push these rights back decades...... I look forward to the Disabled Workers' Committee continuing to work together with the Women's Committee on this and other areas of common interest.

STUC Disabled Workers' Committee
Chair, Barbra Farmer, PCS, at STUC Women's Conference 2012

The STUC Archive

73 Delegates attend Founding Congress - Glasgow 1897

The story of how this representation has changed over the past 116 years and more can be found in the STUC Archive.

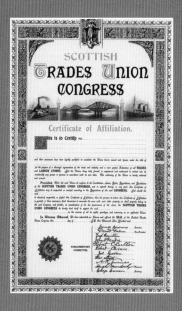

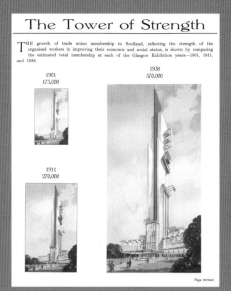

Records of the Scottish Trades Union Congress are held at Glasgow Caledonian University Archives.

The STUC is an organisation of primarily Scottish, but also of UK and indeed international importance. The STUC Archive provides a very comprehensive coverage of all its many areas of activity from its foundation in 1897 to the present day. It is an eclectic collection not purely tied to Scottish labour history, but a resource rich in social history and the development of a nation. From the earliest days, the Congress concerned itself with a wide range of economic and social questions, the Scottish economy and wider issues concerning the people of Scotland. It holds fascinating information on many of the major historical and political events from the end of the 19th century to the present day.

It also has an international thread, given the STUC's input in international affairs over the years. The Archive, housed at Glasgow Caledonian University, is 170 linear metres in size and is made up of paper records, audio visual material, posters, badges, photographs, artefacts, displays, banners and ephemera.

To find out more about the collection please visit:
www.gcu.ac.uk/archives/stuc/
Carole McCallum
University Archivist
e. C.McCallum@gcu.ac.uk
t. 0141 273 1188

Images opposite:
Delegates at first Congress, 1897.
STUC Certificate of Affiliation.
The Tower of Strength diagram, STUC Souvenir Programme for 1938.

Trade Union Contacts

Accord
www.accord-myunion.org
AEGIS the Union
www.aegistheunion.co.uk
Associated Society of Locomotive Engineers & Firemen
www.aslef.org.uk
Association of Educational Psychologists
www.aep.org.uk
Bakers, Food & Allied Workers Union
www.bfawu.org
British Airline Pilots' Association
www.balpa.org
The British Dietetic Association
www.bda.uk.com
British and Irish Orthoptic Society
www.orthoptics.org.uk
Broadcasting, Entertainment, Cinematograph & Theatre Union
www.bectu.org.uk
Chartered Society of Physiotherapy
www.csp.org.uk
Communication Workers' Union
www.cwu.org
Community
www.community-tu.org
Educational Institute of Scotland
www.eis.org.uk
Equity
www.equity.org.uk
FDA
www.fda.org.uk
Fire Brigades Union
www.fbu.org.uk
GMB
www.gmb.org.uk
Hospital Consultants & Specialists Association
www.hcsa.com
Musicians Union
www.theMU.org
NASUWT
www.nasuwt.org.uk

National Union of Journalists
www.nuj.org.uk
National Union of Mineworkers: Scotland Area
www.num.org.uk
National Union of Rail, Maritime & Transport Workers
www.rmt.org.uk
Nautilus International
www.nautilus-intl.com
NUM: COSA
t. 01623 559444
Prison Officers' Association (Scotland)
www.poauk.org.uk
Prospect
www.prospect.org.uk
Public and Commercial Services Union
www.pcs.org.uk
Scottish Secondary Teachers' Association
www.ssta.org.uk
Scottish Society of Playwrights
www.scottishsocietyofplaywrights.co.uk
Society of Chiropodists & Podiatrists
www.scpod.org
Society of Radiographers
www.sor.org
Transport Salaried Staffs' Association
www.tssa.org.uk
Union of Construction, Allied Trades & Technicians
www.ucatt.org.uk
Union of Shop, Distributive & Allied Workers
www.usdaw.org.uk
UNISON
www.unison-scotland.org.uk
Unite the Union
www.unitetheunion.com
United Road Transport Union
www.urtu.com
University and College Union
www.ucu.org.uk/scotland

Details correct as of November 2013

Some sources for further information

Gallacher Memorial Library
www.gcu.ac.uk/specialcollections/collections/gml

Glasgow Women's Library
www.womenslibrary.org.uk

Mapping Memorials to Women inScotland
www.womenofscotland.org.uk

National Library of Scotland
www.nls.uk

National Mining Museum Scotland
www.scottishminingmuseum.com

Remember Mary Barbour
www.remembermarybarbour.com

The STUC Archives Glasgow Caledonian University
www.gcu.ac.uk/archives/stuc/

Trades Union Congress Library Collections
www.londonmet.ac.uk/services/sas/library-services/tuc

TUC History Online
www.unionhistory.info

The Wick Society
www.wickheritage.org
www.johnstoncollection.net

Women's History Scotland
www.womenshistoryscotland.org

The Scottish Trades Union Congress the first 80 years 1897-1977
Angela Tuckett, Mainstream Publishing 1986.

The Bairns O'Adam the Story of the STUC 1897-1997
Keith Aitken, Polygon, Edinburgh 1997.

The Biographical Dictionary of Scottish Women
Ed Elizabeth Ewan, Sue Innes, Sian Reynolds. Co-ordinating Editor, Rose Pipes Edinburgh. University Press 2007.

Credits

Page 2 Agendas from the STUC Archives, Glasgow Caledonian University.
Page 9 STUC Archives, Glasgow Caledonian University.
Page 10 From an EIS publication October 2009, to mark the 'Gude Cause' commemorative events.
Page 13 Image of text from John Murray, The General Strike of 1926, pub 1951, Lawrence and Wishart Ltd. Photograph from National Mining Museum of Scotland collection. West of Scotland Powerloom Weavers card: TUC Archives, from collection at National Library of Scotland.
Page 14 Image Glasgow Caledonian University Archives: Gallacher Memorial Library Collection.
Page 15 Photograph Glasgow Caledonian University Archives: The Gallacher Memorial Library Collection.
Page 16 Photograph by kind permission of the Wick Society, Johnston Collection. Text from Scottish Union Learning.
Page 17 STUC Archives, Glasgow Caledonian University.
Page 20, 21, 22 Article thanks to Jane McKay.
Page 22 By kind permission Jane McKay.
Page 23, 38, 44 Equal Voice was produced by the STUC Women's Committee from 1986 -1995.
Page 24 Photographs Des Loughney.
Page 28 Photograph Glasgow Caledonian University Archives: Gallacher Memorial Library Collection.
Page 29 Images STUC Archives, Glasgow Caledonian University.

Page 31 Woolworths poster from TUC Archives, copyright USDAW. Extract from Equal Opportunities Commission commemorative publication 2005. Card designed by Anne McChlery for Scottish Women's Aid 1980s.
Page 32 Photograph provided by Glasgow Trades Union Council.
Page 35 Image from Glasgow District Trades Council Annual Report 1984-85.
Page 35, 36 Article thanks to Ella Egan.
Page 37 Photograph from National Mining Museum Scotland collection.
Page 42, 43 Photographs Alan Wylie.
Page 48, 49 STUC Archives, Glasgow Caledonian University.
Page 53 In November 1997 STUC Women's Conference in Dundee marked the STUC centenary with a procession to call for 50/50 representation in the new Scottish Parliament. Photographs Alan Richardson Photography.
Page 55 STUC Archives, Glasgow Caledonian University.
Page 59 Photographs Margaret Ferguson Burns, Gude Cause Project.
Page 63 Photograph STUC.
Page 64 Photograph UNISON.
Page 65 Photograph Louis Flood.
Page 66 First photograph STUC, second photograph Louis Flood.
Page 67 Photograph STUC.
Page 68 Photograph Louis Flood.
Page 72, 73 Photographs Louis Flood.

Thanks

Thanks go to the following unions for financial support in the early stages of the project: CWU Scottish Women's Regional Committee; EIS; GMB Scotland; GMB Glasgow General APEX Branch; PCS; UNITE (Scottish Region) and to all those that have contributed images and information throughout the project.

Our thanks to Carole McCallum at the STUC Archives, Glasgow Caledonian University for her assistance and encouragement.

Thanks also go to all the STUC Women's Committee members and STUC staff, past and present, who have assisted, in particular to Helen Carson for the ongoing support provided to the Committee.

Thanks are also to be recorded to Sharon Edwards (PCS), Ella Egan, Ronnie McDonald, and Jane McKay for their contributions.